THE
YALE SERIES OF YOUNGER POETS

SPIRES AND POPLARS

AMS PRESS
NEW YORK

Spires and Poplars

ALFRED R. BELLINGER

NEW HAVEN · YALE UNIVERSITY PRESS
LONDON · HUMPHREY MILFORD · OXFORD UNIVERSITY PRESS
MDCCCCXX

811
B44ᴅ

Reprinted with permission of Yale University Press
From the edition of 1920, New Haven
First AMS EDITION published 1971
Manufactured in the United States of America

International Standard Book Number:
  Complete Set: 0-404-53800-2
  Volume 4: 0-404-53804-5

Library of Congress Card Catalog Book Number: 72-144711

A

AMS PRESS, INC.
NEW YORK, N.Y. 10003

CONTENTS.

5

1917–1919.

J. C. F.

THESE songs of France are little worth
    Unless it be to one who knew
  The various soil from which they grew,
The melancholy and the mirth,
Strange plenitude and stranger dearth
    That lent their influence unto
      These songs of France.

Then take them, John, who saw their birth,
    For none can know so well as you
  How out of blood and out of dew
There blossomed on that sacred earth
      These songs of France.

I.

THE harbor lights through which we find
  Our passage to the distant land
Shine on a cold and silent strand;
With sombre clouds the night is blind.
Yet what are dark and cold combined
  Those flames of magic to withstand,
      The harbor lights?

Now be we all of joyous mind,
  Swift to obey or to command!
  The great adventure is at hand—
Yonder is France that looms behind
      The harbor lights!

II.

AUSTERE and gray the walls without;
  Within, a quietness that glows
With heavenly colors all about,
  With gorgeous blue and gold and rose.
  The ancient columns seem to doze
That guard so sure, so silently,
This dim cathedral sanctity.

With song, with clamor and with shout
  Down the long street the column goes:
Here kneel the weary and devout.
  The winter sun descending throws
  Its rays through wondrous glass that shows
Old saints who still benignant see
This dim cathedral sanctity.

This is no time for sloth or doubt;
  We may not dally with repose.
The day needs zealous men and stout,
  With faces set against our foes.
  Yet, when the work is done—who knows?
Eternity itself may be
This dim cathedral sanctity.

III.

THE new year comes with wind and snow.
  As up the silent street we go
  The day has dawned; the wearied men
Against the gale are bending low
  And stumbling blindly now and then.

What lies before we may not know
But we must forward even so,
  For it were shame to falter when
    The new year comes.

In spite of all the winds that blow,
In spite of every doubt and woe
  And dangers still beyond our ken,
  We lift us and take heart again,
For with the eastern hills aglow,
    The new year comes.

IV.

WE live at ease behind the lines
    Where death and battle come not nigh.
The walls are hung with glossy vines,
    The branches of the trees on high
    Make tracery against the sky,
The rue is green in every crack,
    And all is lovely to the eye—
But, oh, the women clad in black!

Beneath the shadow of the pines
    A single golden butterfly
Makes mock of winter, and the signs
    Of spring abundant we descry.
    Violets in the meadows lie,
Daisies bedeck the shepherd's track,
    And all things war and cold defy—
But, oh, the women clad in black!

Yet idleness the soul confines
    More straitly than with chains. We sigh
To quit this beauty that combines
    To lull our hearts to sloth. Ah, why
    Are we not to the north to try
Our mettle? If we come not back—
    We have eternity to buy—
But, oh, the women clad in black!

    Courage to peril makes reply
And, God be thanked, there are no lack
    Of men who do not fear to die!
But, oh, the women clad in black!

V.

Among the solemn cypress trees
  The redbreasts' song is blithe and clear.
Enough of bitter threnodies
Among the solemn cypress trees!
More fit that on white days like these
  Above the dead who slumber here
Among the solemn cypress trees
  The redbreasts' song is blithe and clear.

VI.

You who have held your head so proudly high
  Nor grudged the cost, nor dallied with desire,
  You to whose gallantry we all aspire,
Who laugh and suffer with undaunted eye,
We should be shamed to temporize or sigh
  Seeing you strong to what the fates require—
You who have held your head so proudly high
  Nor grudged the cost, nor dallied with desire.
May the good time of peace be very nigh
  When he whose love and life are yours entire
  Shall come from out his test of blood and fire
And find, when bitter warfare has passed by,
You who have held your head so proudly high.

VII.

ATHWART the ruddy dawn
   The singing skylarks soar.
The morning mists are drawn
Athwart the ruddy dawn.
The peaceful night is gone—
   And man goes forth to war.
Athwart the ruddy dawn
   The singing skylarks soar.

VIII.

O BEAUTIFUL and reckless whom I loved,
  Dead while your life was strong with youth and pride!
  Were it not better had a thousand died
Than you, with all your promises unproved?
Full debonair and modest as behoved
  A gallant gentleman, as yet untried,
O beautiful and reckless whom I loved,
  Dead while your life was strong with youth and pride!
Through perils, eager, unafraid you roved
  Seeking your star and turning not aside.
  Now you are gone but still there shall abide
Sunshine about the places where you moved,
O beautiful and reckless whom I loved.

IX.

THE almond tree has blossomed out
  In spite of winter and of wind.
Better its flowered faith and blind
Than bare discretion born of doubt.
Let him that would misfortune flout
  Look to the hills, and he shall find
    The almond tree.

Who would suspect a heart so stout
  In that frail stem for spring designed—
  For spring, whose coming sure and kind
Is heralded in white about
    The almond tree.

X.

A LONELY wooden cross
　Upon a foreign soil
Is all that marks my loss.
A lonely wooden cross
Among the pines that toss
　In ceaseless, fruitless toil.
A lonely wooden cross
　Upon a foreign soil.

XI.

Now God be thanked the spring has come again,
   And all the hope and happiness of spring
After these weary months of sullen rain
   Have leapt to life at the year's blossoming.
   Oh, hark! the season's tender heralding
Where, half uncertain, from the hedge hard by
   The reminiscent birds begin to sing;
For song is holy and can never die.

Our hearts that through these winter months have lain
   Passive and dumb to aught that life could bring
Beat nobly in their old accustomed strain
   Before the magic of that carolling.
   Winter and weariness are on the wing,
The winds with music have swept clear the sky,
   The very trees make music as they swing,
For song is holy and can never die.

Yet war is ever present and its pain,
   Sorrow and loss have still their ancient sting,
The menace and the tragedy remain.
   The foe advancing, commoner and king,
   Trample our fanes and grim defiance fling
To God and man. Our steadfast hearts and high
   With song move forward to his chastening,
For song is holy and can never die.

   What though should perish every lovely thing
That man hath made his heart to gratify?
   They still should live for man's remembering
For song is holy and can never die.

XII.

WE laughed and parted, nevermore to meet
    In this fair world of April green and blue.
The whimsical companionship was through,
The gay, light-hearted interlude complete.
Rising from the green bank that was our seat,
    Jesting at life, as we were wont to do,
We laughed and parted, nevermore to meet
    In this fair world of April green and blue.
Why did I never say how passing sweet
    Had been the days that I had spent with you?
    I almost thought you felt the impulse too—
The chance was gone, and, rising to our feet,
We laughed and parted, nevermore to meet.

XIII.

THE sun in heaven is bright
   On fields with clover gay.
After the breathless fight
The sun in heaven is bright,
And his benignant light
   Covers the dead today.
The sun in heaven is bright
   On fields with clover gay.

XIV.

THIS palace gods might make their throne
   And in these gardens take their ease.
How kingly sumptuous the stone
   Among the ancient guardian trees!
   But, oh, more excellent than these
The sweet contentment of the sky,
The all but summer of Versailles!

We, happily, have never grown
   Too worn upon by life to seize
Such fleeting moments of our own
   To live eternal harmonies.
   This charm all apprehension flees
And weariness is banished by
The all but summer of Versailles.

Tomorrow each must go alone
   To what the fates of war shall please.
The shadow of the vague unknown
   Lies yonder. Though our victories
   Be bought with many tragedies
We shall remember, you and I,
The all but summer of Versailles.

XV.

BRIGHT as a single poppy in a field
  This perfect afternoon has been to me,
  Breaking the long days of monotony
As with a flash of scarlet. It shall yield
Full many a song whose music lay concealed
  Until this magic moment set it free.
Bright as a single poppy in a field
  This perfect afternoon has been to me,
For where the summer woodland made a shield
  Against the jargon of humanity
  I looked beneath the veil of tragedy
And saw immortal gaiety revealed
Bright as a single poppy in a field.

XVI.

THE day he died, that last triumphant day,
    Found him untainted with the thought of fear,
  Facing the sudden death that crashed so near
Supremely lovable, supremely gay,
How buoyant and how swift! Who would not pray
    So to burst into Heaven with a cheer!
The day he died, that last triumphant day,
    Found him untainted with the thought of fear.
How can we pity him of whom men say
    "Our bravest and our best is fallen here"?
    Ah, we are proud of him, who held him dear,
And we remember that he led the way
The day he died, that last triumphant day.

XVII.

In calm and ancient dignity the Seine
  Sweeps through the town of towns beneath the bow
Of many a bridge, and, with a half disdain,
  Ripples about their massive piers below,
  Confined, yet patient to endure it so.
On either border of its mighty swell
  The art of ages flourishes I know,
But I love best the gentle voiced Moselle.

The broad Garonne moves silent to the main
  And lingers all along its course as though
It loved the vanished highlands and were fain
  To shun the roar and hurry of Bordeaux.
  There rise the poplar trees in stately row
And cast upon the soul a subtle spell
  With weaving of their branches to and fro,
But I love best the gentle voiced Moselle.

Unhurried through the heart of the Touraine
  The lordly Loire's historic waters flow,
And sing in proud and reminiscent strain
  The deathless glories of the high châteaux.
  With old romance the valley is aglow
For there the unforgotten splendors dwell
  And great traditions of the long ago—
But I love best the gentle voiced Moselle.

Upon the fruitful bosom of the plain
  In spring beside the upper Marne they sow.
The summer makes it glorious with grain
  And flowered loveliness the meadows show.
  Along the stream the scented breezes blow,
The blossoms of the field are sweet to smell,
  And sweet the fragrance of the grass they mow.
But I love best the gentle voiced Moselle.

With mingled memories of pride and pain
  The Meuse moves seaward, tortuous and slow,

Forever dreaming of the bitter gain
    Of those bare ruins, purchased with our woe,
    Silent save where the melancholy crow
Flaps on above that long extinguished hell,
    While on our dead the trees their blossoms strow.
But I love best the gentle voiced Moselle.

Time was when wild and bloody ran the Aisne
    To witness the confusion of the foe,
And never shall the stream forget that stain
    Though whitened with a thousand winters' snow.
    Here too lie our heroic dead, and, oh,
We love the spot. Forever where they fell
    Memorials of scarlet poppies grow.
But I love best the gentle voiced Moselle.

    Ah, streams of France, your varied beauties throw
Their charm about my heart: I love you well.
    On each his excellence the gods bestow
But I love best the gentle voiced Moselle.

XVIII.

H ERE once a village stood
  That was the home of men
Who lived when God was good.
Here once a village stood,
And all this blasted wood
  Was green with summer then.
Here once a village stood
  That was the home of men.

XIX.

IN honor and in triumph, O my friend,
Your soul has gone beyond my mortal view
And left me with the poignant need of you
Which later fellowships can never mend.
I prayed, with you beside me to ascend
The heights of life. We should have won thereto
In honor and in triumph. O my friend,
Your soul has gone beyond my mortal view.
Yet, to my spirit still your soul shall lend
Courage and strength. Clear eyed, as you would do,
I face the challenge of my life anew,
And know that you will meet me in the end
In honor and in triumph, O my friend.

XX.

THE wood of Apremont is still and cold,
   Its laughing leaves are dust, its birds are fled,
And never shall it echo as of old
   To rustle and to piping overhead.

Autumn has come with russet and with red;
Evening has come with glory and with gold.
   They cannot exorcise the chill and dread.
The wood of Apremont is still and cold.

Beneath its leaves quaint tales and gay were told,
   Within its shades what tender words were said
What time the black thrush sang! But now, behold,
   Its laughing leaves are dust, its birds are fled.

Its noons were noisy with the children's tread,
Its evenings sang of lovers as they strolled.
   But now is only silence and the dead,
And never shall it echo as of old.

The spring shall find it blasted trunks and mold
   And weeds on ruin and corruption fed.
Anemones shall nevermore unfold
   To rustle and to piping overhead.

But God who counteth blood that hath been shed,
Whom naught escapeth, sad or base or bold,
   Shall give to it eternity instead,
And in the woods of heaven shall be enrolled
      The wood of Apremont.

XXI.

THOSE ruined walls of stone
  Had been the house of prayer.
The weeds had overgrown
Those ruined walls of stone,
But I went in alone
  Awhile to worship there.
Those ruined walls of stone
  Had been the house of prayer.

XXII.

A YEAR ago on Hempstead plain
    Across the snow the wind was keen,
  And bitter little gusts would glean
Dead leaves where, in the quiet lane,
With memories of summer rain
    Under the hedge the grass was green
        A year ago. .

Oh, would that I might once again
    Breathe in that wind so white and clean!
    I was at peace, I had not seen
This dreary dwelling place of pain
        A year ago.

XXIII.

I LOVED her for the laughter in her eyes
  Which all the world at war could not subdue.
   Life's glory and life's bitterness she knew,
And hopeless dawns and vivid noonday skies
Were in the texture of her spirit, wise
   And calm and gay as the eternal blue.
I loved her for the laughter in her eyes
   Which all the world at war could not subdue.
O splendid alchemy that could surprise
   The brightness of existence shining through
   Its chaos and its clouds, and so make true
The golden hope of joy that in us lies.
I loved her for the laughter in her eyes.

XXIV.

THE distant cannons' steady roar
  Last night was loud, and now they cease!
How strange that we shall hear no more
The distant cannons' steady roar!
For we have grown so used to war;
  So inconceivable is peace.
The distant cannons' steady roar
  Last night was loud, and now—they cease.

XXV.

SLEEP in this sacred earth, the strife is done.
   Failure and triumph both are laid to rest
   Upon the all-forgiving mother's breast
In equal peace beneath the kindly sun.
Never again shall trumpet call or gun
   Arouse you to take up the bitter quest.
Sleep in this sacred earth, the strife is done.
   Failure and triumph both are laid to rest.
Save God himself alone there now is none
   Who can divide the baser from the best
   Or weigh the worth of the unworthiest.
But they that hopeless fought and they that won
Sleep in this sacred earth. The strife is done.

XXVI.

Is it not strange that by this shore
  We two should walk together thus
  And all in idleness discuss
The pleasant days that are no more,
We who, a little time before,
    Counted these lands half fabulous?
        Is it not strange?

Dreadful to many is the score
    Of battle, aye, and onerous,
    But when such times recall to us
The fruit that we have reaped of war—
        Is it not strange?

XXVII.

THIS land of vivid skies and sparkling seas
    Blue beyond all imagining of blue!
This land of oranges upon the trees
    More golden than the fabled fruit that grew
    In the Hesperides! Can it be true
That we have lived to see the struggle cease,
    That clouds and battle are transmuted to
The gaiety of Christmas and of Nice?

How wonderful to wander at our ease
    With none to watch or hinder what we do!
Here are no testy godlings to appease,
    No fruitless, empty labors to eschew;
    No purpose but our fancies to pursue,
Our duty to give thanks for our release
    And, every splendid hour, to prove anew
The gaiety of Christmas and of Nice.

Care is a monster, doubt is a disease
    And melancholy but a witches' brew.
This is no time for phantoms such as these.
    Myrtle and roses mingle not with rue.
    Let us forget awhile! Our hours are few.
Let song arise and revelry increase.
    'Twere shame to own that retrospection slew
The gaiety of Christmas and of Nice!

Yet—friends too long unseen, the sight of you
    Here in the glory of the reborn peace
Runs like a theme of deep thanksgiving through
    The gaiety of Christmas and of Nice.

XXVIII.

WE three before an open fire
    Holding the sum of man's desire
  Can warm our hands and laugh at fate,
  For this serene triumvirate
Has all that mortal could require.

We touch the long forgotten lyre
And day's crude clamorings retire,
  While happy on the Muses wait
    We three.

The war's last flickerings expire.
With its monotony and mire
  Perish its tragedy and hate.
  And now—old thoughts and old debate,
And, seeking visions new and higher,
    We three.

XXIX.

MON père, incomparable host,
    Surely it comes to very few
  So broadly and so deep to view
Your France. I with your eyes, I boast,
A little saw, rejoicing most
    To find the eyes so wise and true,
        Mon père.

I drink—my heart is in the toast—
    To youth perpetual for you.
    Rich be your joys and ever new,
Speedy your advent to our coast,
        Mon père.

XXX.

Old ivy covered walls of gray
   That guard this dear secluded lane,
Stand ye immutable for ay,
Old ivy covered walls of gray.
I take my leave of you today,
  But I will surely come again,
Old ivy covered walls of gray
   That guard this dear secluded lane.

XXXI.

Southward beside the Rhone in spring we sped,
The river, turbulent and swollen, fed
  By melting snows from hills to left and right.
  Far off rose one indomitable height
Ice crowned, but winter's mastery was dead,
And lusty breezes from the sea had bred
New leaves and blossoms by the river bed.
    And gay we journeyed, gladdened by the sight,
        Southward beside the Rhone.

Behind, the river dwindled to a thread.
The sunset stained its yellow waters red;
  The hills were touched with an unearthly light;
  And still we sped beneath the coming night,
With hearts and faces toward the sea ahead,
        Southward beside the Rhone.

XXXII.

BEHIND us faint and fainter grows the shore
 That was the whole of life to us of late.
The sky is blue, and blue the waves that roar
 And beckon us with laughter where they wait.
 The breezes freshen to felicitate
Our outward passage to the sunlit sea,
For we are going home triumphantly!
 Yet, as the prow slips sweetly through the tide,
 We check our eagerness to turn aside
A moment for one half regretful glance—
One moment of affection and of pride:
The time has come to bid farewell to France.

A little while and all that went before
 Of pain and passion, weariness and hate
Shall be forgotten; we shall feel once more
 Old hopes revive, old labors fascinate.
 But this our parting we would dedicate
Unto a life that now has ceased to be,
And live again in this brief memory
 Our perils passed, our handicaps defied,
 The bitterness wherewith our souls were tried,
And, over all, the bloom and the romance,
 The splendid vision that shall still abide
Beyond the time to bid farewell to France.

Not all return, for some there be who bore
 The burden well, whose staunchness made us great,
Who fainted not in the long strain of war
 Nor flinched in battle, loud, precipitate,
 Hot, overwhelming as the face of Fate;
And from its midst were suddenly set free
Into the quiet of eternity.
 Theirs is the light, which died not when they died,
 Which serves our generation as its guide;
Theirs is the glorious inheritance
 To sleep, eternal comrades, side by side,
And nevermore to bid farewell to France.

O sister land! Whate'er the years may hide
Our common blood shall never be denied.
Eager we came to thy deliverance,
 And, as we leave thee, wiser, clearer eyed
We bid thee hail and then farewell, O France!

POEMS TO SEVERAL PEOPLE.

F. P. M.

O Icarus, incarnate soul of flight,
Insatiate of swiftness and of height,
Fit comrade of the lark whose heart of fire
Springs up ecstatic in a wild desire
To quench the sun with song! To thee the sky
Was home, the winds that laugh so sweet on high
Gave eager welcome to thy kindred soul
And thou, as Heaven itself had been thy goal,
Up, up, and up in joyous fearlessness
Wast wont to circle. Who can ever guess
What blithe companionship with voiceless space
Was thine in that free solitary race—
What jocund converse with the sun by day
And with the stars upon the milky way
When thou wouldst seek for stardust at its source
And fragrant night was cold about thy course?
Flying itself was very life to thee,
So dear that nothing but eternity
Could tempt thee from it. Now thy flight is o'er.
The summer sky shall never see thee more
After that day when from a cloudy rift
Thou divedst down to soar again more swift
Than ever man has flown, in Heaven's light
To satiate thy soul with perfect height
O Icarus—thou disembodied flight!

M. M. H.

Do you remember when the spring was young
The mornings when we walked abroad to see
The little tender leaves upon the tree
New green and all with tiny dewdrops hung?

Do you remember how the birds would sing
And how the river in an undertone
Laughed to itself, how bright the morning shone
And every cloudlet seemed a living thing?

Those days are gone and cannot come again—
Those light and pleasant days. From such as they,
The essence of an evanescent May
Departed utterly, what can remain?

Only the songs that never can be sung,
The fragrance of imperishable flowers,
Only the memory of golden hours
And spotless mornings when the spring was young.

H. P. P.

OUR time was almost ended
  And we were left alone.
O, half uncomprehended
  And yet most truly known,

I who am still your debtor
  In silence took your hand.
How could I thank you better,
  Knowing you understand?

You burst my life asunder
  With your fantastic soul,
Your weariness and wonder,
  Your bitter wit and droll;

Insulting dawn with sadness,
  Shocking the night with cheers
And with a jocund madness
  Breathlessly close to tears.

Pain have I known and pleasure,
  Laughter and war and woe,
And yet your spirit's treasure
  I can but dimly know.

Your spirit is a jewel
  Of fierce and lovely lights,
Of tender flames and cruel,
  Of awful depths and heights.

You scorn and fear tomorrow,
  You mock and long for rest.
All life is in your sorrow,
  All death is in your jest.

But, heart beyond my knowing,
  Yet closer to my heart
Than all your overflowing
  Of fantasy and art,

49

Though all our laughter perish
  When all our tears are dead,
We still shall have to cherish
  The words we left unsaid.

To speak would be to cheapen
  The things we cannot tell
Which silence would but deepen—
  Hail, brother, and farewell!

H. P.

THEY were new buds, the leaves that now are falling,
   When last we met; they find us, I am sure,
Unchanged at heart as now we sit recalling
   That distant other world of ours at Tours.

What motley whims and fancies to remember!
   The antic revels that were our delight,
The fascination of the dying ember
   And golden laughter in the winter night.

In future years of too infrequent meeting
   Can any of that recollection last?
Surely the sight of you, however fleeting,
   Will always call to mind that vivid past.

I still must pay, whatever comes hereafter,
   My homage to a faith that will not tire—
A heart to turn the winter night to laughter
   And glorify the glow of dying fire.

C. L. W., WITH A MIRROR.

Last year, as tribute to your gallant heart,
  Our scanty best of offerings we brought
To you, and you with a surpassing art
  Made rich by your acceptance things of naught.

And I had nothing but my idle days—
  My gray and idle days to bring you there.
Yet you transformed the empty gifts in ways
  Most wonderful, to make them passing fair.

Yours was a magic to outlast the war,
  A power to be perpetually true.
And so, behold, I bring to you once more
  A gift to be made beautiful by you.

Z. S., JULY, 1917.

THE single lamp that lights the quiet room
    Sends ruddy rays athwart the outer gloom
      Where trees are motionless against the sky
And, underneath, the roses are in bloom.

Thus sitting we can almost catch once more
The old content we knew so well before
      Our academic peace was split in twain
And we were burst upon by sudden war.

The old content! Withdrawing for a space
From every contact with our time and place
      To be familiars of the kings of men
And meet the godlike heroes face to face.

Thoughts of tomorrow's cares and tasks to drown
How often have we talked the planets down
      While lights upon the campus one by one
Went out, and all was silent in the town.

The nights when our philosophy was wrought
By subtle skill of language and of thought
      Into vague likeness of eternal truth—
What fool shall say that they were spent for naught?

What shall our later lives' fruition show
That was not there innate, for even so
      The seed contains the rose that is to be—
Who knows in what strange fields the rose will blow?

What sorcery is here that makes this night
Unlike the bygone times of our delight
      When poetry made rich the printed page
And stately visions rose upon our sight?

The hours with Homer and with Sophocles
Were peaceful hours and sweet. Yet are not these
      As peaceful? Lo, the stars are in the sky
And roses blooming underneath the trees.

53

The change is not about us but within,
For we have felt the will to war begin
   And, in this matching of titanic powers,
We know that to be idle were to sin.

And we are full of newborn restlessness,
Unsatisfied to praise and to profess,
   Eager to prove us strong to give our all
Or know ourselves for nothing, being less.

It matters not what foe or folly saith.
That lives today which late was but a wraith:
   The transubstantiation hath been wrought—
The wine of creed is made the blood of faith.

Friend of the best of these my younger days,
Sharer alike of labors and of praise,
   The dayspring of our comradeship is past
And we are at the parting of the ways.

War is a fickle master at the best
And may divide us far as east from west.
   Who knows what nights like this may bring us soon,
What weariness and bitter need of rest?

Lo, we are caught in world-compelling powers.
Yet still the memory of other hours
   Shall fall upon my soul in nights to come
Refreshing as the starlight on the flowers.

And you, although perchance your task be set
In some far place beyond my vision, yet—
   We two together saw the bloom of life
And well I know that you will not forget.

For this is not forever. Though it be
The greatest thing our lives should ever see,
   War is ephemeral. But still abide
The things we loved unto eternity.

In spite of all the agony and scars
That are the substance and the fruit of wars
    The roses in the night are not less sweet
Nor skies less spacious nor less white the stars.

So joy remembered is forever new.
Wherefore, in spite of all that time can do,
    What we have lived time cannot take away,
And life will still be rich because of you.